# Awesome Keto Vegetarian Recipes

**Quick, Easy and Delicious Recipes for a Plant-Based Ketogenic Diet**

*Lidia Wong*

# TABLE OF CONTENTS

# INTRODUCTION

The keto diet is the shortened term for ketogenic diet and it is essentially a high-fat and low-carb diet that helps you lose weight, thereby bringing various health benefits. This diet drastically restricts your carb intake while increasing your fat intake; this pushes your body to go into a state know as "*ketosis*". We will tackle ketosis in a bit.

The human body uses glucose from carbs to fuel metabolic pathways—meaning various bodily functions like digestion, breathing, etc.. Essentially, anything that needs energy. Even when you are resting, the body needs fuel or energy for you to continue living. If you think about it, when have you ever stopped breathing, or your heart stopped beating, or your liver stopped from cleansing the body, or your kidneys from filtering blood?

Never, unless you're dead, which is the only time in which the body doesn't need energy. In normal circumstances, glucose is the primary pathway when it comes to sourcing the body's energy.

But the body also has another pathway; it can utilize fats to fuel the various bodily processes. And this is what we call "*ketosis*". And the body can only enter ketosis when there is no glucose available, thus the reason for sticking to a low-carb diet is essential in the keto diet. Since no glucose is available, the body is pushed to use fats—it can either come from the food you consume or from your body's fat reserves—the adipose tissue or from the flabby parts of your body. This is how the keto diet helps you lose weight, by burning up all those stored fats that you have and using it to fuel bodily processes.

That said, if for whatever reason you are a vegetarian, following a ketogenic diet can be extremely difficult. A vegetarian diet is largely free of animal products, which means that food tends to be usually high in carbohydrates. Still, with careful planning, it is possible. This Cookbook will provide you with various easy and delicious dishes to help you stick to your ketogenic diet plan while being a vegetarian.

Enjoy!

# Keto Pumpkin Pancakes

Preparation Time: 10 minutes

Cooking Time: 6 minutes

Servings: 8

## Ingredients:

- 2 large eggs
- 2 tablespoons butter
- 1 teaspoon pumpkin spice
- 1 teaspoon baking powder
- ¼ cup sour cream
- 1 cup almond meal
- ¼ cup pumpkin puree
- 1/4 teaspoon salt

## Directions:

1. First, in a mixing bowl combine your eggs, sour cream and butter.
2. In another mixing bowl, combine salt, almond meal, spice, baking powder.
3. Now slowly add your wet ingredients to your dry ingredients, while stirring to blend.
4. This will give you a sweet, smooth batter.
5. Over medium-heat warm up a cast-iron frying pan and grease it with butter.
6. Pour about 1/3 of your mixture into the skillet.

7. When bubbles begin to form on top of the batter, allow it to cook for about another minute, then flip it over.
8. Cook on the other side for an additional minute or so.
9. Repeat the previous last two steps until your batter is done.
10. Serve up your keto pumpkin pancakes with your favorite toppings.

**Nutritional Values (Per Serving):**

Calories: 150, Fat: 11 g, Carbs: 1.5 g, Protein: 5.5 g

# Greens and Olives Pan

Preparation time: 10 minutes

Cooking time: 15 minutes

Servings: 4


## Ingredients:

- 4 spring onions, chopped
- 2 tablespoons olive oil
- ¼ cup pine nuts, toasted
- ½ cup green olives, pitted and halved
- 1 tablespoon balsamic vinegar

- 2 cups baby spinach
- 1 cup baby arugula
- 1 cup asparagus, trimmed, blanched and halved
- Salt and black pepper to the taste

## Directions:

1. Heat up a pan with the oil over medium high heat, add the spring onions and the asparagus and sauté for 5 minutes.
2. Add the olives, spinach and the other ingredients, toss, cook over medium heat for 10 minutes, divide between plates and serve for lunch.

## Nutrition:

calories 136, fat 13.1, fiber 1.9, carbs 4.4, protein 2.8

# Roasted Bok Choy and Sprouts Mix

Preparation time: 10 minutes

Cooking time: 30 minutes

Servings: 4

## Ingredients:

- 2 tablespoons olive oil
- ½ pound bok choy, torn
- 1 pound Brussels sprouts, trimmed and halved
- 1 tablespoon garlic powder
- 1 tablespoon chili powder
- 2 tablespoons balsamic vinegar
- 1 tablespoon onion powder
- A pinch of salt and black pepper
- 1 teaspoon sweet paprika

## Directions:

1. In a roasting pan, combine the bok choy with the sprouts, the oil and the other ingredients, toss and cook at 390 degrees F for 30 minutes.
2. Divide the mix between plates and serve right away.

## Nutrition:

calories 100, fat 2, fiber 2, carbs 9, protein 1

# Tomato Cucumber Cheese Salad

Preparation Time: 15 minutes

Servings: 2

## Ingredients:

- 2 cups tomatoes, sliced
- 2 cucumbers, peeled, sliced
- 7-ounces mozzarella cheese, chopped
- 2 spring onions, sliced

- 12 black olives
- 2 teaspoons basil pesto
- 2 tablespoons extra-virgin olive oil
- 2 tablespoons basil, fresh, chopped

## Directions:

1. In a large salad bowl, add basil pesto and cheese.
2. Mix well.
3. Add remaining ingredients into a bowl and toss to blend.
4. Serve fresh and enjoy!

## Nutritional Values (Per Serving):

Calories: 609 Fat: 50.5 g Carbohydrates: 13.7 g
Sugar: 7.5 g Protein: 27.2 g Cholesterol: 47 mg

# Broccoli Omelet

Preparation Time: 10 minutes

Cooking Time: 10 minutes

Servings: 2

## Ingredients:

- 4 eggs, organic
- 1 tablespoon extra-virgin olive oil
- 1 cup broccoli, cooked, chopped

- 1 tablespoon parsley, chopped
- ½ teaspoon sea salt
- ¼ teaspoon pepper

## Directions:

1. In a mixing bowl, beat eggs with salt and pepper. Add broccoli to egg mixture.
2. Heat the olive oil in a pan over medium heat.
3. Pour your broccoli and eggs mixture into the pan and cook until set.
4. Flip and cook other side until lightly browned.
5. Garnish with chopped parsley.
6. Serve and joy!

## Nutritional Values (Per Serving):

Calories: 203 Fat: 15.9 g Cholesterol: 327 mg Protein: 12.4 g Carbohydrates: 4 g Sugar: 1.5 g

# Eggplant Pomodoro

Preparation Time: 5 min

Cooking Time: 15 min

Serves: 4

## Ingredients:

- 1 Medium Eggplant, diced
- ½ cup Black Olives, sliced
- 1 cup Diced Tomatoes
- 4 cloves Garlic, minced
- 2 tbsp Red Wine Vinegar
- pinch of Red Pepper Flakes
- 2 tbsp Olive Oil
- Salt and Pepper to taste
- 4 cups Shirataki Pasta
- Fresh Parsley for garnish

## Directions:

1. Heat olive oil in a pan.
2. Sautee garlic and red pepper flakes until aromatic.

3. Add eggplants, tomatoes, olives and red wine vinegar.
4. Stir until eggplants are soft.
5. Toss shirataki into the pan.
6. Season with salt and pepper.
7. Garnish with chopped fresh parsley for serving.

## Nutritional Values:

Kcal per serve: 101 Fat: 7 g. Protein: 1 g. Carbs: 9 g.

# Vegetable Char Siu

Preparation Time: 5 min

Cooking Time: 15 min

Serves: 4

## Ingredients:

- 100 grams Raw Jackfruit, deseeded and rinsed
- 50 grams Red Bell Pepper, cut into thin strips
- 100 grams Cucumbers, cut into thin strips
- 2 cloves Garlic, minced
- 1 Shallot, minced
- ¼ cup Char Siu Sauce
- ¼ cup Water
- 2 tbsp Peanut Oil

## Directions:

1. Heat peanut oil in a pan.
2. Add jackfruit and stir until slightly brown.
3. Add garlic and shallots and sautee until aromatic.

4. Add water and char siu sauce. Simmer until jackfruit is tender.
5. Shred jackfruit with forks.
6. Toss in cucumbers and bell peppers.


**Nutritional Values:**

Kcal per serve: 100 Fat: 7 g. Protein: 1 g. Carbs: 9 g.

# Mini Vegetable Quiche

Preparation Time: 30 minutes

Servings: 12

## Ingredients:

- 7 eggs
- 1/4 cup bell pepper, diced
- 1/4 cup onion, chopped
- 1/4 cup mushroom, diced

- 3/4 cup cheddar cheese, shredded
- 10 oz frozen spinach, chopped

## Directions:

1. Line muffin cups with aluminum foil cups set aside.
2. Add all ingredients into the large bowl and beat lightly to combine.
3. Pour egg mixture into the prepared muffin tray.
4. Bake at 350 $^0$F for 20 minutes.
5. Serve warm and enjoy.

## Nutritional Value (Amount per Serving):

Calories 73 Fat 5 g Carbohydrates 1 g Sugar 0.6 g Protein 5 g Cholesterol 103 mg

# Tempeh Zucchini Mug Melt

Preparation Time: 5 minutes

Cooking Time: 2 minutes

Serving: 2

## Ingredients:

- 4 slices cooked tempeh
- 3 tbsp sour cream
- 1 small zucchini, chopped
- Salt and black pepper to taste
- 2 tbsp chopped green chilies
- 3 oz shredded Monterey Jack cheese

## Directions:

1. Divide the tempeh slices in the bottom of two wide mugs and carefully spread with 1 tablespoon of sour cream.
2. Top with the zucchini, season with salt and black pepper, add the green chilies, and top with the remaining sour cream and then the Monterey Jack cheese.

3. Place the mugs in the microwave and cook for 1 to 2 minutes or until the cheese melts.
4. Remove the mugs; allow cooling for 1 minute, and serve.

## Nutrition:

Calories:136, Total Fat: 9.6g, Saturated Fat: 5.2g, Total Carbs: 5 g, Dietary Fiber: 2g, Sugar: 1g, Protein: 9g, Sodium: 253mg

# Kale and Mushroom Pierogis

Prep Time:15 minutes

Cooking Time: 30 minutes

Serving: 4

**Ingredients:**

*For the stuffing:*

- 2 tbsp butter
- 2 garlic cloves, finely chopped
- 1 small red onion, finely chopped
- 3 oz. baby bella mushrooms, sliced
- 2 oz. fresh kale
- ¼ tsp black pepper
- ½ tsp salt
- ½ cup cashew cream
- 2 oz. grated tofu cheese

*For the pierogi:*

- 1 tbsp flax seed powder + 3 tbsp water
- 4 tbsp coconut flour
- ½ cup almond flour
- ½ tsp salt
- 1 tsp baking powder

- 1½ cups shredded tofu cheese
- 5 tbsp butter
- Olive oil for brushing

## Directions:

1. Put the butter in a skillet and melt over medium heat, then add and sauté the garlic, red onion, mushrooms, and kale until the mushrooms brown.
2. Season the mixture with salt and black pepper and reduce the heat to low. Stir in the cashew cream and tofu cheese and simmer for 1 minute. Turn the heat off and set the filling aside to cool.
3. Make the pierogis: In a small bowl, mix the flax seed powder with water and allow sitting for 5 minutes.
4. In a bowl, combine the almond flour, coconut flour, salt, and baking powder.
5. Put a small pan over low heat, add, and melt the tofu cheese and butter while stirring continuously until smooth batter forms. Turn the heat off.

6. Pour the flax egg into the cream mixture, continue stirring, while adding the flour mixture until a firm dough forms.
7. Mold the dough into four balls, place on a chopping board, and use a rolling pin to flatten each into ½ inch thin round pieces.
8. Spread a generous amount of stuffing on one-half of each dough, then fold over the filling, and seal the dough with your fingers.
9. Brush with olive oil, place on a baking sheet, and bake for 20 minutes or until the pierogis turn a golden brown color.
10. Serve the pierogis with a lettuce tomato salad.

## Nutrition:

Calories:364, Total Fat:33.4 g, Saturated Fat:17.3 g, Total Carbs:8g, Dietary Fiber:2g, Sugar:3 g, Protein:12 g, Sodium:779 mg

# Balsamic Kale

Preparation time: 10 minutes

Cooking time: 20 minutes

Servings: 4

**Ingredients:**

- 1 pound kale, torn
- 1 tablespoon balsamic vinegar
- 2 tablespoons walnuts, chopped

- 1 tablespoon olive oil
- 1 teaspoon cumin, ground
- 1 teaspoon chili powder
- 3 garlic cloves, minced
- 2 tablespoons cilantro, chopped

## Directions:

1. Heat up a pan with the oil over medium heat, add the garlic and the walnuts and cook for 2 minutes.
2. Add the kale, vinegar and the other ingredients, toss, cook over medium heat for 18 minutes more, divide between plates and serve as a side.

## Nutrition:

calories 170, fat 11, fiber 3, carbs 7, protein 7

# Cabbage and Green Beans

Preparation time: 10 minutes

Cooking time: 15 minutes

Servings: 4

## Ingredients:

- 1 green cabbage head, shredded
- 2 cups green beans, trimmed and halved
- 1 teaspoon sweet paprika
- 2 tablespoons olive oil
- 1 teaspoon cumin, ground
- Salt and black pepper to the taste
- 1 tablespoon chives, chopped

## Directions:

1. Heat up a pan with the oil over medium heat, add the cabbage and the paprika and sauté for 2 minutes.
2. Add the green beans and the other ingredients, toss, cook over medium heat for 13 minutes more, divide between plates and serve.

## Nutrition:

calories 200, fat 4, fiber 2, carbs 3, protein 7

# Garlic Cauliflower Rice

Preparation time: 10 minutes

Cooking time: 20 minutes

Servings: 4

## Ingredients:

- 2 cups cauliflower rice
- 2 tablespoons almonds, chopped
- 2 green onions, chopped

- 1 tablespoon olive oil
- 4 garlic cloves, minced
- 3 tablespoons chives, chopped
- ½ cup vegetable stock

## Directions:

1. Heat up a pan with the oil over medium heat, add the garlic and green onions and sauté for 5 minutes.
2. Add the cauliflower rice and the other ingredients, toss, cook over medium heat for 15 minutes, divide between plates and serve.

## Nutrition:

calories 142, fat 6.1, fiber 1.2, carbs 3, protein 1.2

# Kale and Tomatoes

Preparation time: 5 minutes

Cooking time: 20 minutes

Servings: 4

**Ingredients:**

- 1 cup cherry tomatoes, halved
- 1 yellow onion, chopped
- 1 pound baby kale
- 2 tablespoons olive oil

- 1 tablespoon balsamic vinegar
- 1 tablespoon cilantro, chopped
- 2 tablespoons vegetable stock
- A pinch of salt and black pepper

## Directions:

1. Heat up a pan with the oil over medium heat, add the onion and sauté for 5 minutes.
2. Add the kale, tomatoes and the other ingredients, toss, cook over medium heat for 15 minutes more, divide between plates and serve as a side dish.

## Nutrition:

calories 170, fat 6, fiber 6, carbs 9, protein 4

# Mushrooms and Black Beans

Preparation time: 10 minutes

Cooking time: 25 minutes

Servings: 4


## Ingredients:

- 1 pound mushrooms, sliced
- 1 yellow onion, chopped
- 1 teaspoon cumin, ground
- 1 teaspoon sweet paprika
- 1 cup canned black beans, drained and rinsed
- 2 tablespoons olive oil
- ½ cup chicken stock
- A pinch of salt and black pepper
- 2 tablespoons cilantro, chopped


## Directions:

1. Heat up a pan with the oil over medium heat, add the onion and sauté for 5 minutes.
2. Add the mushrooms and sauté for 5 minutes more.

3. Add the rest of the ingredients, toss, cook over medium heat for 15 minutes more.
4. Divide everything between plates and serve as a side dish.
5. Enjoy!

**Nutrition:**

calories 189, fat 3, fiber 4, carbs 9, protein 8

# Scalloped Potatoes

Preparation time: 10 minutes

Cooking time: 4 hours

Servings: 8

**Ingredients:**

- Cooking spray
- 1 yellow onion, cut into medium wedges
- 2 pounds gold potatoes, halved and sliced
- 10 ounces canned vegan potato cream soup
- 8 ounces coconut milk
- 1 cup tofu, crumbled
- ½ cup veggie stock
- Salt and black pepper to the taste
- 1 tablespoons parsley, chopped

**Directions:**

1. Coat your slow cooker with cooking spray and arrange half of the potatoes on the bottom.
2. Layer onion wedges, half of the vegan cream soup, coconut milk, tofu, stock, salt and pepper.

3. Add the rest of the potatoes, onion wedges, cream, coconut milk, tofu and stock, cover and cook on High for 4 hours.
4. Sprinkle parsley on top, divide scalloped potatoes between plates and serve as a side dish.
5. Enjoy!

**Nutrition:**

calories 306, fat 14, fiber 4, carbs 30, protein 12

# Acorn Squash And Great Sauce

Preparation time: 10 minutes

Cooking time: 6 hours

Servings: 4

## Ingredients:

- 2 acorn squash, halved, deseeded and cut into medium wedges
- ¼ cup raisins
- 16 ounces cranberry sauce
- ¼ cup orange marmalade
- A pinch of salt and black pepper
- ¼ teaspoon cinnamon powder

## Directions:

1. In your slow cooker, mix squash with raisins, cranberry sauce, orange marmalade, salt, pepper and cinnamon powder, toss, cover and cook on Low for 6 hours.
2. Stir again, divide between plates and serve as a side dish.
3. Enjoy!

## Nutrition:

calories 325, fat 6, fiber 3, carbs 28, protein 3

# Hot Okra

Preparation time: 10 minutes

Cooking time: 20 minutes

Servings: 4

**Ingredients:**

- 1 pound okra, halved
- 4 scallions, chopped
- 2 tablespoons avocado oil
- 2 garlic cloves, minced

- 1 tablespoon chili powder
- 1 tablespoon balsamic vinegar
- 1 teaspoon hot paprika
- A pinch of salt and black pepper

**Directions:**

1. Heat up a pan with the oil over medium heat, add the scallions and the garlic and sauté for 5 minutes.
2. Add the okra and the other ingredients, toss, cook over medium heat for 15 minutes, divide between plates and serve as a side dish.

**Nutrition:**

calories 182, fat 4, fiber 2, carbs 6, protein 6

# Steamed Cauliflower

Preparation time: 5 minutes

cooking time: 10 minutes

servings: 6

## Ingredients

- 1 large head cauliflower
- ½ teaspoon salt
- 1 cup water
- 1 teaspoon red pepper flakes (optional)

## Directions

1. Remove any leaves from the cauliflower, and cut it into florets.
2. In a large saucepan, bring the water to a boil. Place a steamer basket over the water, and add the florets and salt.
3. Cover and steam for 5 to 7 minutes, until tender.
4. In a large bowl, toss the cauliflower with the red pepper flakes (if using).
5. Transfer the florets to a large airtight container or 6 single-serving containers.
6. Let cool before sealing the lids.

## Nutrition:

Calories: 35; Fat: 0g; Protein: 3g; Carbohydrates: 7g; Fiber: 4g; Sugar: 4g; Sodium: 236mg

# Sicilian Stuffed Tomatoes

Preparation time: 10 minutes

cooking time: 30 minutes

servings: 4

## Ingredients

- 2 cups water
- 1 cup couscous
- 3 green onions, minced
- 1/3 cup golden raisins
- 4 large ripe tomatoes
- 1 teaspoon finely grated orange zest
- Salt
- 1/3 cup toasted pine nuts
- 1/4 cup minced fresh parsley
- Freshly ground black pepper
- 2 teaspoons olive oil

## Directions

1. Preheat the oven to 375 °F. Lightly oil a 9 x 13-inch baking pan and set aside. In a large saucepan, bring the water to a boil over high

heat. Stir in the couscous and salt to taste and remove from the heat.

2. Stir in the green onions, raisins, and orange zest.
3. Cover and set aside for 5 minutes.
4. Cut a 1/2-inch-thick slice off the top of each of the tomatoes. Scoop out the pulp, keeping the tomato shells intact.
5. Chop the pulp and place it in a large bowl.
6. Add the couscous mixture along with the pine nuts, parsley, and salt and pepper to taste. Mix well.
7. Fill the tomatoes with the mixture and place them in the prepared pan.
8. Drizzle the tomatoes with the oil, cover with foil, and bake until hot, about 20 minutes.
9. Serve immediately.

# Maple Glazed Carrots

Preparation time: 10 minutes

Cooking time: 15 minutes

Servings: 4


**Ingredients:**

- 1 pound carrots, sliced
- 1 tablespoon ghee
- 1 tablespoon coconut oil

- ½½ teaspoon nutmeg
- cup pineapple juice
- 1 teaspoon ginger, grated
- ½ tablespoon maple syrup
- 1 tablespoon parsley, chopped

## Directions:

1. Heat a pan with the ghee and the oil over medium-high heat, add ginger, stir and cook for 2 minutes.
2. Add carrots, stir and cook for 5 minutes.
3. Add pineapple juice, maple syrup and nutmeg, stir and cook for 5 minutes more.
4. Add parsley, stir, cook for 3 minutes, divide between plates and serve.
5. Enjoy!

## Nutritional value/serving:

calories 130, fat 6,8, fiber 3, carbs 17,4, protein 1,1

# Superb Lemon Roasted Artichokes

Preparation Time: 10 mins

Servings: 2

## Ingredients

- 2 peeled and sliced garlic cloves
- 3 lemon pieces
- 2 artichoke pieces
- Black pepper
- 3 tbsps. olive oil
- Sea flavored vinegar

## Directions:

1. Wash your artichokes well and dip them in water and cut the stem to about ½ inch long
2. Trim the thorny tips and outer leaves and rub the chokes with lemon
3. Poke garlic slivers between the choke leaves and place a trivet basket in the Cooker then add artichokes
4. Lock up the lid and cook on high pressure for 7 minutes

5. Release the pressure naturally over 10 minutes
6. Transfer the artichokes to a cutting board and allow them to cool then cut half lengthwise and cut the purple white center
7. Pre-heat your oven to 400 degrees Fahrenheit
8. Take a bowl and mix 1 and ½ lemon and olive oil
9. Pour over the choke halves and sprinkle flavored vinegar and pepper
10. Place an iron skillet in your oven and heat it up for 5 minutes
11. Add a few teaspoons of oil and place the marinated artichoke halves in the skillet
12. Brush with lemon and olive oil mixture
13. Cut third lemon in quarter and nestle them between the halves
14. Roast for 20-25 minutes until the chokes are browned
15. Serve and enjoy!

**Nutrition:**

Calories: 263, Fat:16 g, Carbs:8 g, Protein:23 g, Sugars:128 g, Sodium:0.4 mg

# Minted Peas Feta Rice

Preparation Time: 15 mins

Servings: 2

## Ingredients:

- 1 ¼ c. vegetable broth
- ¾ c. sliced scallions
- 1 ½ c. frozen peas
- ¾ c. brown rice
- ¼ c. finely crumbled feta cheese
- Freshly ground pepper
- ¼ c. sliced fresh mint

## Directions:

1. Boil broth in a saucepan over medium heat.
2. Add rice and bring it to a simmer. Cook for 4 minutes.
3. Stir in peas and cook for 6 minutes.
4. Turn off the heat then add feta, mint, scallions, and pepper.
5. Serve warm.

## Nutrition:

Calories: 28.1, Fat:18.2 g, Carbs:10.3 g, Protein:8.8 g, Sugars:2.2 g, Sodium:216 mg

# Apples and Cabbage Mix

Preparation Time: 5 mins

Servings: 4


## Ingredients:

- 2 cored and cubed green apples
- 2 tbsps. balsamic vinegar
- ½ tsp. caraway seeds
- Black pepper
- 2 tbsps. olive oil
- 1 shredded red cabbage head


## Directions:

1. In a bowl, combine the cabbage with the apples and the other ingredients, toss and serve.


## Nutrition:

Calories: 165, Fat:7.4 g, Carbs:26 g, Protein:2.6 g, Sugars:2.6 g, Sodium:19 mg

# Creamy Asparagus

Preparation time: 10 minutes

Cooking time: 15 minutes

Servings: 3

## Ingredients:

- 10 ounces asparagus spears, cut into medium-sized pieces, and steamed
- 2 tablespoons Parmesan cheese, grated
- ⅓ cup Monterey jack cheese, shredded

- Salt and ground black pepper, to taste
- 2 tablespoons mustard
- 2 ounces cream cheese
- ⅓ cup heavy cream
- 3 tablespoons bacon, cooked and crumbled

## Directions:

1. Heat up a pan with the mustard, heavy cream, and cream cheese over medium heat and stir well.
2. Add the Monterey Jack cheese, and Parmesan cheese, stir, and cook until it melts.
3. Add the half of the bacon, and the asparagus, stir, and cook for 3 minutes.
4. Add the rest of the bacon, plus salt and pepper, stir, cook for 5 minutes, divide on plates, and serve.

## Nutrition:

Calories - 256, Fat - 23, Fiber - 2, Carbs - 5, Protein - 13

# Creamy Radishes

Preparation time: 10 minutes

Cooking time: 25 minutes

Servings: 1


## Ingredients:

- 7 ounces radishes, cut in half
- 2 tablespoons sour cream
- 1 tablespoon green onion, peeled and chopped
- 1 tablespoon cheddar cheese, grated
- 2 bacon slices
- Hot sauce, to taste
- Salt and ground black pepper, to taste


## Directions:

1. Put the radishes into a pot, add the water to cover, bring to a boil over medium heat, cook them for 10 minutes, and drain.
2. Heat up a pan over medium-high heat, add the bacon, cook until crispy, transfer to paper towels, drain the grease, crumble, and leave aside.

3. Return the pan to medium heat, add the radishes, stir, and sauté them for 7 minutes.
4. Add the onion, salt, pepper, hot sauce, and sour cream, stir, and cook for 7 minutes.
5. Transfer to a plate, top with crumbled bacon and cheddar cheese, and serve.


**Nutrition:**

Calories - 340, Fat - 23, Fiber - 3, Carbs - 6, Protein - 15

# Avocado and Cucumber Salad

Preparation time: 10 minutes

Cooking time: 0 minutes

Servings: 4

## Ingredients:

- 1 onion, peeled and sliced
- 1 cucumber, sliced
- 2 avocados, pitted, peeled, and chopped
- ¼ cup fresh cilantro, chopped
- 2 tablespoons lemon juice
- 1 pound cherry tomatoes, halved
- 2 tablespoons olive oil
- Salt and ground black pepper, to taste

## Directions:

1. In a large salad bowl, mix the tomatoes with the cucumber, onion, and avocado, and stir.
2. Add the oil, salt, pepper, and lemon juice, and toss to coat well.
3. Serve cold with cilantro on top.

## Nutrition:

Calories - 140, Fat - 4, Fiber - 2, Carbs - 4, Protein - 5

# Swiss Chard and Chicken Soup

Preparation time: 10 minutes

Cooking time: 35 minutes

Servings: 12

## Ingredients:

- 4 cups Swiss chard, chopped
- 4 cups chicken breast, cooked, and shredded
- 1 cup mushrooms, sliced
- 1 tablespoon garlic, minced
- 2 cups water
- 1 tablespoon coconut oil, melted
- ¼ cup onion, peeled and chopped
- 8 cups chicken stock
- 1 cup green beans, cut into medium-sized pieces
- 2 cups yellow squash, chopped
- 2 tablespoons vinegar
- ¼ cup fresh basil, chopped
- Salt and ground black pepper, to taste
- 4 bacon slices, chopped
- ¼ cup sundried tomatoes, cored and chopped

## Directions:

1. Heat up a pot with the oil over medium-high heat, add the bacon, stir, and cook for 2 minutes.
2. Add the tomatoes, garlic, onions, and mushrooms, stir, and cook for 5 minutes.
3. Add the water, stock, and chicken, stir, and cook for 15 minutes.
4. Add the Swiss chard, green beans, squash, salt, and pepper, stir, and cook for 10 minutes.
5. Add the vinegar, basil, salt, and pepper, stir, ladle into soup bowls, and serve.

## Nutrition:

Calories - 140, Fat - 4, Fiber - 2, Carbs - 4, Protein - 18

# Roasted Vegetable Bisque

Preparation time: 10 minutes

cooking time: 15 minutes

servings: 6

## Ingredients

- 1 large onion, coarsely chopped
- 2 medium carrots, coarsely chopped
- 1 large russet potato, peeled and cut into 1/2-inch dice
- 1 large ripe tomato, quartered
- 1 medium zucchini, thinly sliced
- 2 garlic cloves, crushed
- 2 tablespoons olive oil
- 1/2 teaspoon dried savory
- 1/2 teaspoon dried thyme
- Salt and freshly ground black pepper
- 4 cups vegetable broth, homemade (see Light Vegetable Broth or store-bought, or water)
- 1 tablespoon minced fresh parsley, for garnish

## Directions

1. Preheat the oven to 400 °F. In a lightly oiled 9 x 13-inch baking pan, place the onion, carrots, potato, zucchini, tomato, and garlic. Drizzle with the oil and season with savory, thyme, and salt and pepper to taste. Cover tightly with foil and bake until softened, about 30 minutes. Uncover and bake, stirring once, until vegetables are lightly browned, about 30 minutes more.

2. Transfer the roasted vegetables to a large soup pot, add the broth, and bring to a boil. Reduce the heat to low and simmer, uncovered, for 15 minutes.

3. Puree the soup in the pot with an immersion blender or in a blender or food processor, in batches if necessary, and return to the pot. Heat over medium heat until hot. Taste, adjusting seasonings if necessary.

4. Ladle into bowls, sprinkle with parsley, and serve.

# Pomegranate-Infused Lentil And Chickpea Stew

Preparation time: 5 minutes

cooking time: 55 minutes

servings: 4

## Ingredients

- ¾ cup brown lentils, picked over, rinsed, and drained
- ¾ cup long-grain brown rice
- 2 tablespoons olive oil
- 1/2 cup chopped green onions
- 2 teaspoons minced fresh ginger
- 1/2 cup dried apricots, quartered
- 1/4 cup golden raisins
- 1/4 teaspoon ground allspice
- 1 teaspoon turmeric
- 1/4 teaspoon ground cumin
- 1/4 teaspoon ground cayenne
- Salt and freshly ground black pepper
- 1/3 cup pomegranate molasses, homemade (recipe follows or store-bought)
- 3 cups water

- 11/2 cups cooked or 1 (15.5-ouncecan chickpeas, drained and rinsed
- 1/4 cup minced fresh cilantro or parsley

## Directions

1. Soak the lentils in a medium bowl of hot water for 45 minutes. Drain and set aside.
2. In a large saucepan, heat the oil over medium heat. Add the green onions, ginger, soaked lentils, rice, apricots, raisins, allspice, cumin, cayenne, turmeric, and salt and pepper to taste. Cook, stirring, for 1 minute.
3. Add the pomegranate molasses and water and bring to a boil. Reduce heat to low. Cover and simmer until the lentils and rice are tender, about 40 minutes.
4. Stir in the chickpeas and cilantro. Simmer, uncovered, for 15 minutes, to heat through and allow the flavors to blend. Serve immediately.

# Ethiopian Cabbage, Carrot, and Potato Stew

Preparation time: 10 minutes

cooking time: 20 minutes

servings: 6

## Ingredients

- 3 russet potatoes, peeled and cut into ½-inch cubes
- 6 carrots, peeled, halved lengthwise, and cut into ½-inch slices
- 2 tablespoons olive oil
- 1 onion, chopped
- 1 tablespoon ground turmeric
- 1 teaspoon ground cumin
- 4 garlic cloves, minced
- 1 teaspoon ground ginger
- 1½ teaspoons sea salt
- 1½ cups low-sodium vegetable broth, divided
- 4 cups shredded or thinly sliced green cabbage

## Directions

1. Bring a large pot of water to a boil over medium-high heat.

2. Add the potatoes and cook for 10 minutes, or until fork-tender. Drain and set aside. While the potatoes are cooking, heat the oil in a large skillet over medium-high heat. Add the carrots and onion and sauté for 5 minutes. Add the garlic, turmeric, cumin, ginger, and salt and sauté for 1 additional minute, until fragrant. Add the cooked potatoes and 1 cup of broth to the skillet, bring to a boil, and reduce to a simmer. Scatter the cabbage on top of the potatoes. Cover and simmer for 3 minutes.

3. Mix the cabbage into the potatoes, add the remaining ½ cup of broth, cover, and simmer for 5 more minutes, or until the cabbage is wilted and tender. Stir the cabbage from time to time while cooking to incorporate it with the other ingredients as it continues to wilt.

# Zucchini And Butter Bean Bisque

Preparation time: 5 minutes

cooking time: 45 minutes

servings: 4 to 6

## Ingredients

- 2 tablespoons olive oil
- 1 medium onion, chopped
- 1 garlic clove, minced
- 2 cups fresh or frozen butter beans or lima beans
- 3 medium zucchini, cut into 1/4-inch slices
- 1/2 teaspoon dried marjoram
- 4 cups vegetable broth, homemade (see Light Vegetable Broth or store-bought, or water
- Salt and freshly ground black pepper
- 1/2 cup plain unsweetened soy milk
- 2 tablespoons minced jarred pimiento

## Directions

1. In a large soup pot, heat the oil over medium heat. Add the onion and garlic, cover, and cook

until softened, about 5 minutes.

2. Add the butter beans and the broth. Cover and cook for 20 minutes.

3. Add the zucchini, marjoram, and salt and pepper to taste.

4. Bring to a boil, then reduce heat to low and simmer, covered, until the vegetables are soft, about 20 minutes.

5. Puree the soup in the pot with an immersion blender or in a blender or food processor, in batches if necessary, and return to the pot.

6. Stir in the soy milk and taste, adjusting seasonings if necessary. Reheat over low heat until hot.

7. Ladle into bowls, garnish with the pimiento, and serve.

# Autumn Medley Stew

Preparation Time: 5 Minutes

Cooking Time: 60 Minutes

Servings:4 To 6

**Ingredients**

- 2 tablespoons olive oil
- 1 small butternut squash, peeled, halved, seeded, and cut into 1/2-inch dice
- 8 ounces seitan, homemade or store-bought, cut in 1-inch cubes
- Salt and freshly ground black pepper
- 2 garlic cloves, minced
- 1 large yellow onion, chopped
- 1 large russet potato, peeled and cut into 1/2-inch dice
- 1 medium carrot, cut into 1/4-inch dice
- 1 medium parsnip, cut into 1/4-inch dice chopped
- 1 small head savoy cabbage, chopped
- 1 (14.5-ounce) can diced tomatoes, drained
- 11/2 cups cooked or 1 (15.5-ounce) can chickpeas, drained and rinsed

- 2 cups vegetable broth,
- 1/2 cup dry white wine
- 1/2 teaspoon dried marjoram
- 1/2 teaspoon dried thyme
- 1/2 cup crumbled angel hair pasta

## Directions

1. In a large skillet, heat 1 tablespoon of the oil over medium-high heat.
2. Add the seitan and cook until browned on all sides, about 5 minutes.
3. Season with salt and pepper to taste and set aside.
4. In a large saucepan, heat the remaining 1 tablespoon oil over medium heat.
5. Add the onion and garlic. Cover and cook for until softened, about 5 minutes.
6. Add the potato, carrot, parsnip, and squash. Cover and cook until softened, about 10 minutes.
7. Stir in the cabbage, tomatoes, chickpeas, broth, wine, marjoram, thyme, and salt and pepper to taste.

8. Bring to a boil, then reduce heat to low.

9. Cover and cook, occasionally stirring, until the vegetables are tender, about 45 minutes.

10. Add the cooked seitan and the pasta and simmer until the pasta is tender and the flavors are blended, about 10 minutes longer.

11. Serve immediately.

12. Variation: Leave out the pasta and serve with some warm crusty bread.

# Seitan-Asparagus Shirataki Mix

Preparation Time: 40 minutes

Serving: 4

## Ingredients:

*For the angel hair shirataki:*

- 2 (8 oz) packs angel hair shirataki

*For the seitan-asparagus base:*

- 1 lb seitan
- 3 tbsp olive oil
- 2 large shallots, finely chopped
- 1 lb fresh asparagus, cut into 1-inch pieces
- 3 garlic cloves, minced
- Salt and black pepper to taste
- 1 cup finely grated parmesan cheese for topping

## Directions:

*For the angel hair shirataki:*

1. Bring 2 cups of water to a boil in a medium pot over medium heat.
2. Strain the shirataki pasta through a colander and rinse very well under hot running water.
3. Drain properly and transfer the shirataki pasta into the boiling water. Cook for 3 minutes and

strain again.

4. Place a dry large skillet over medium heat and stir-fry the shirataki pasta until visibly dry, 1 to 2 minutes. Take off the heat and set aside.

*For the seitan -asparagus base:*

5. Heat a large non-stick skillet over medium heat and add the seitan. Cook while breaking the lumps that form until brown, 10 minutes. Use a slotted spoon to transfer the seitan to a plate and discard the drippings.

6. Heat the olive oil in the skillet and sauté the asparagus until tender, 5 to 7 minutes. Stir in the shallots and garlic and cook until fragrant, 2 minutes. Season with salt and black pepper.

7. Stir in the seitan, shirataki and toss until well combined. Adjust the taste with salt and black pepper as desired.

8. Dish the food onto serving plates and garnish generously with the parmesan cheese.

9. Serve warm.

**Nutrition:**

Calories:413, Total Fat:30.6g, Saturated Fat:12.3g, Total Carbs: 8g, Dietary Fiber:2g, Sugar: 4g, Protein:5 g, Sodium:37 mg

# Delicious Sambal Seitan Noodles

Preparation Time: 60 minutes

Serving: 4

## Ingredients:

*For the shirataki noodles:*

- 2 (8 oz) packs Miracle noodles, garlic and herb
- Salt to season

*For the sambal seitan:*

- 1 tbsp olive oil
- 1 lb seitan
- 4 garlic cloves, minced
- 1 tsp liquid erythritol
- 1-inch ginger, peeled and grated
- 1 tbsp sugar-free tomato paste
- 2 fresh basil leaves + extra for garnishing
- 2 tbsp sambal oelek
- 2 tbsp plain vinegar
- 1 cup water
- 2 tbsp coconut aminos
- Salt to taste
- 1 tbsp unsalted butter

## Directions:

*For the shirataki noodles:*

1.  Bring 2 cups of water to a boil in a medium pot over medium heat.
2.  Strain the Miracle noodles through a colander and rinse very well under hot running water.
3.  Allow proper draining and pour the noodles into the boiling water. Cook for 3 minutes and strain again.
4.  Place a dry skillet over medium heat and stir-fry the shirataki noodles until visibly dry, 1 to 2 minutes.
5.  Season with salt, plate and set aside.

*For the seitan sambal:*

6.  Heat the olive oil in a large pot and cook in the seitan until brown, 5 minutes.
7.  Stir in the garlic, ginger, liquid erythritol and cook for 1 minute.
8.  Add the tomato paste, cook for 2 minutes and mix in the basil, sambal oelek, vinegar, water, coconut aminos, and salt.
9.  Cover the pot and continue cooking over low heat for 30 minutes.

10. Uncover, add the shirataki noodles, butter and mix well into the sauce.
11. Dish the food, garnish with some basil leaves and serve warm.

## Nutrition:

Calories:538, Total Fat:41.1g, Saturated Fat:16.2g, Total Carbs:20g, Dietary Fiber:14g, Sugar:5g, Protein:29g, Sodium:640mg

# Lemongrass Tempeh with Spaghetti Squash

Preparation Time: 1 hour + 45 minutes marinating time

Serving size: 4

**Ingredients:**

*For the lemongrass tempeh:*

- 2 tbsp minced lemongrass
- 2 tbsp fresh ginger paste
- 2 tbsp sugar-free maple syrup
- 2 tbsp coconut aminos
- 4 tempeh
- 1 tbsp Himalayan salt
- 2 tbsp avocado oil

*For the squash noodles:*

- 3 lb spaghetti squashes, halved and deseeded
- 1 tbsp olive oil
- Salt and black pepper to taste

*For the steamed spinach:*

- 1 tbsp avocado oil
- 1 lb baby spinach

- 1 tsp fresh ginger paste

*For the peanut-coconut sauce:*

- ½ cup coconut milk
- ¼ cup organic almond butter

## Directions:

*For the lemongrass tempeh:*

1. In a medium bowl, mix the lemongrass, ginger paste, maple syrup, coconut aminos, and Himalayan salt. Place the tempeh in the liquid and coat well. Allow marinating for 45 minutes.
2. After, heat the avocado oil in a large skillet, remove the tempeh from the marinade and sear in the oil on both sides until golden brown and cooked through, 10 to 15 minutes. Transfer to a plate and cover with foil.

*For the spaghetti squash:*

3. Preheat the oven to 380 $^0$F.
4. Place the spaghetti squashes on a baking sheet, brush with the olive oil and season with salt and black pepper. Bake in the oven for 20 to 25 minutes or until tender.
5. When ready, remove the squash and shred with

two forks into spaghetti-like strands. Keep warm in the oven.

*For the spinach:*

6. In another skillet, heat the avocado oil and sauté the ginger until fragrant. Add the spinach and cook to wilt while stirring to be coated well in the ginger, 2 minutes. Turn the heat off.

*For the almond-coconut sauce:*

7. In a medium bowl, quickly whisk the coconut milk with the almond butter until well combined.

*To serve:*

8. Unwrap and divide the tempeh into four bowls, add the spaghetti squash to the side, then the spinach and drizzle the almond sauce on top.
9. Serve immediately.


**Nutrition:**

Calories:457, Total Fat:37g, Saturated Fat:8.1g, Total Carbs:17g, Dietary Fiber:5g, Sugar:4g, Protein:22g, Sodium:656mg

# Brussels sprouts Salad

Preparation Time: 20 minutes

Cooking Time: 0 minutes

Servings: 6

## Ingredients:

- 1 ½ lbs Brussels sprouts, trimmed
- ¼ cup toasted hazelnuts, chopped
- 1 ½ tbsp lemon juice
- 2 tsp Dijon mustard
- 2 tbsp olive oil
- Pepper
- Salt

## Directions:

1. In a small bowl, whisk together oil, mustard, lemon juice, pepper, and salt.
2. In a large bowl, combine together Brussels sprouts and hazelnuts.
3. Pour dressing over salad and toss well.
4. Serve immediately and enjoy.

## Nutrition:

Calories 111 Fat 7.1 g Carbohydrates 11 g Sugar 2.7 g Protein 4.4 g Cholesterol 0 mg

# Cauliflower Radish Salad

Preparation Time: 15 minutes

Cooking Time: 0 minutes

Servings: 4

## Ingredients:

- 12 radishes, trimmed and chopped
- 1 tsp dried dill
- 1 tsp Dijon mustard

- 1 tbsp cider vinegar
- 1 cup parsley, chopped
- ½ medium cauliflower head, trimmed and chopped
- 1 tbsp olive oil
- ½ tsp black pepper
- ¼ tsp sea salt

## Directions:

1. In a mixing bowl, combine together cauliflower, parsley, and radishes.
2. In a small bowl, whisk together olive oil, dill, mustard, vinegar, pepper, and salt.
3. Pour dressing over salad and toss well.
4. Serve immediately and enjoy.

## Nutrition:

Calories 58 Fat 3.8 g Carbohydrates 5.6 g Sugar 2.1 g Protein 2.1 g Cholesterol 0 mg

# Potato Salad With Artichoke Hearts

Preparation time: 15 minutes

cooking time: 15 minutes

servings: 4 to 6

## Ingredients

- 11/2 pounds Yukon Gold potatoes, peeled and cut into 1-inch dice
- 1 (10-ounce package frozen artichoke hearts, cooked
- 2 cups halved ripe grape tomatoes
- 1/2 cup frozen peas, thawed
- 3 green onions, minced
- 2 tablespoons fresh lemon juice
- 1 tablespoon minced fresh parsley
- 1/3 cup olive oil
- 1 garlic clove, minced
- Salt and freshly ground black pepper

## Directions

1. In a large pot of boiling salted water, cook the potatoes until just tender but still firm, about 15

minutes. Drain well and transfer to a large bowl.

2. Quarter the artichokes and add them to the potatoes. Add the tomatoes, peas, green onions, and parsley and set aside.

3. In a small bowl, combine the oil, lemon juice, garlic, salt, and pepper to taste. Mix well, pour the dressing over potato salad, and toss gently to combine. Set aside at room temperature to allow flavors to blend, about 20 minutes.

4. Taste, adjusting seasonings if necessary, and serve.

# Apple and Ginger Slaw

Preparation Time: 10 Minutes

Cooking Time: 0 Minutes

Servings:4

## Ingredients

- 2 tablespoons olive oil
- 2 apples, peeled and julienned
- juice of 1 lemon, or 2 tablespoons prepared lemon juice
- 1 teaspoon grated fresh ginger
- pinch of sea salt
- 4 cups shredded red cabbage

## Directions

1. In a small bowl, whisk together the olive oil, lemon juice, ginger, and salt and set aside.
2. In a large bowl, combine the apples and cabbage.
3. Toss with the vinaigrette and serve immediately. Store leftovers in an airtight container in the refrigerator for up to 3 days.

# Roasted Potato Salad With Chickpeas And Tomatoes

Preparation Time: 5 Minutes

Cooking Time: 20 Minutes

Servings:4 To 6

## Ingredients

- 11/2 pounds Yukon Gold potatoes, cut into 1/2-inch dice
- 1 medium shallot, halved lengthwise and cut into 1/4-inch slices
- 1/4 cup olive oil
- Salt and freshly ground black pepper
- 3 tablespoons white wine vinegar
- 11/2 cups cooked or 1 (15.5-ounce) can chickpeas, drained and rinsed
- 1/3 cup chopped drained oil-packed sun-dried tomatoes
- 1/4 cup green olives, pitted and halved
- 1/4 cup chopped fresh parsley

## Directions

1. Preheat the oven to 425 °F. In a large bowl, combine the potatoes, shallot, and 1 tablespoon of the oil.
2. Season with salt and pepper to taste and toss to coat.
3. Transfer the potatoes and shallot to a baking sheet and roast, turning once, until tender and golden brown, about 20 minutes.
4. Transfer to a large bowl and set aside to cool.
5. In a small bowl, combine the remaining 3 tablespoons oil with the vinegar and pepper to taste.
6. Add the chickpeas, tomatoes, olives, and parsley to the cooked potatoes and shallots.
7. Drizzle with the dressing and toss gently to combine.
8. Taste, adjusting seasonings if necessary.
9. Serve warm or at room temperature.

# Tomato and Basil Bruschetta

Preparation time: 10 minutes

cooking time: 6 minutes

servings: 12 bruschetta

## Ingredients

- 3 tomatoes, chopped
- 1 baguette, cut into 12 slices
- ¼ cup chopped fresh basil

- 1 tablespoon olive oil
- pinch of sea salt
- 1 garlic clove, sliced in half

## Directions

1. In a small bowl, combine the tomatoes, basil, olive oil, and salt and stir to mix. Set aside. Preheat the oven to 425 °F.
2. Place the baguette slices in a single layer on a baking sheet and toast in the oven until brown, about 6 minutes.
3. Flip the bread slices over once during cooking. Remove from the oven and rub the bread on both sides with the sliced clove of -garlic.
4. Top with the tomato-basil mixture and serve immediately.

# Coriander Mint Chutney

Preparation time: 10 minutes

Cooking time: 12 minutes

Servings: 4

## Ingredients:

- 1 and ½ teaspoons cumin seeds
- 1 and ½ teaspoons garam masala
- 2 tablespoons avocado oil

- ½ teaspoon mustard seeds
- 2 garlic cloves, minced
- ¼ cup veggie stock
- 1 cup mint
- 1 tablespoon ginger, grated
- 2 teaspoons lime juice
- A pinch of salt and black pepper

**Directions:**

1. Heat up a pan with the oil over medium heat, add the cumin, garam masala, mustard seeds, garlic and ginger and cook for 5 minutes.
2. Add the mint and the other ingredients, stir, cook over medium heat for 7 minutes more, divide into bowls and serve as a snack.

**Nutrition:**

calories 241, fat 4, fiber 7, carbs 10, protein 6

# Rosemary Chard Dip

Preparation time: 10 minutes

Cooking time: 20 minutes

Servings: 4

**Ingredients:**

- 4 cups chard, chopped
- 2 cups coconut cream
- ½ cup cashews, chopped
- A pinch of salt and black pepper
- 1 teaspoon smoked paprika
- ½ teaspoon chili powder
- ¼ teaspoon mustard powder
- ½ cup cilantro, chopped

**Directions:**

1. In a pan, combine the chard with the cream, cashews and the other ingredients, stir, cook over medium heat for 20 minutes and transfer to a blender.
2. Pulse well, divide into bowls and serve as a party dip.

**Nutrition:**

calories 200, fat 4, fiber 3, carbs 6, protein 7

# Spanish Vegetable Omelet

Preparation Time: 10 minutes

Cooking Time: 15 minutes

Servings: 4

## Ingredients:

- 6 eggs
- 2 red peppers, chopped in thin strips
- 2 chopped scallions

- 1 diced zucchini
- 3 tbsps. olive oil
- Salt
- Black pepper

**Directions:**

1. Heat the olive oil in a pan; sauté chopped green onions for 3-4 minutes.
2. Add the peppers and cook for about 2 minutes more.
3. Add the zucchini and sauté for another 3 minutes.
4. In a mixing bowl, beat the eggs. Add salt and pepper to taste.
5. Mix the vegetables into the eggs.
6. Heat the olive oil in the frying pan and pour the whisked eggs mixture into the skillet.
7. Cook the omelet for 1 to 2 minutes. Serve hot.

**Nutrition:**

Calories: 0, Fat: 7.53g, Carbs: 6.7, Protein: 10.91g

# Chocolate Ginger Cookies

Preparation time: 10 minutes

Cooking time: 20 minutes

Servings: 6

## Ingredients:

- 2 cups almonds, chopped
- 2 tablespoons flaxseed mixed with 3 tablespoons

water

- ¼ cup avocado oil
- ¼ cup cocoa powder
- 2 tablespoons stevia
- 1 teaspoon baking soda

## Directions:

1. In your food processor, combine the almonds with the flaxseed mix and the other ingredients, pulse well, scoop tablespoons out of this mix, arrange them on a lined baking sheet, flatten them a bit and cook at 360 degrees F for 20 minutes.
2. Serve the cookies cold.

## Nutrition:

calories 252, fat 41.6, fiber 6.5, carbs 11.7, protein 3

# Apricots Cake

Preparation time: 10 minutes

Cooking time: 30 minutes

Servings: 8

## Ingredients:

- ¾ cup stevia
- 2 cups coconut flour
- ½ cup almond milk
- ¼ cup coconut oil, melted

- 1 teaspoon baking powder
- 2 tablespoons flaxseed mixed with 3 tablespoons water
- ½ teaspoon vanilla extract
- Juice of 1 lime
- 2 cups apricots, chopped

## Directions:

1. In a bowl, mix the flour with the coconut oil, the stevia and the other ingredients, whisk and pour into a cake pan lined with parchment paper.
2. Introduce in the oven at 375 degrees F, bake for 30 minutes, cool down, slice and serve.

## Nutrition:

calories 221, fat 8.3, fiber 3.4, carbs 14.5, protein 5

# Dates Mousse

Preparation time: 30 minutes

Cooking time: 0 minutes

Servings: 4

## Ingredients:

- 2 cups dates, chopped
- 2 cups coconut cream
- ¼ cup stevia
- 1 teaspoon almond extract
- 1 teaspoon vanilla extract

## Directions:

1. In a blender, combine the cream with the stevia, dates and the other ingredients, pulse well, divide into cups and keep in the fridge for 30 minutes before serving.

## Nutrition:

calories 141, fat 4.7, fiber 4.7, carbs 8.3, protein 0.8

# Watermelon and Rhubarb Cream

Preparation time: 10 minutes

Cooking time: 0 minutes

Servings: 2

## Ingredients:

- 1 pound watermelon, peeled and chopped
- 1 cup rhubarb, chopped
- 1 cup coconut cream
- 1 teaspoon vanilla extract
- 1 teaspoon lime juice
- 2 teaspoons lime zest, grated

## Directions:

1. In a blender, combine the watermelon with the rhubarb, the vanilla and the rest of the ingredients, pulse well, divide into cups and keep in the fridge before serving.

## Nutrition:

calories 122, fat 5.7, fiber 3.2, carbs 5.3, protein 0.4

# Cocoa Ice Cream

Preparation Time: 10 minutes

Cooking time: 30 minutes

Servings: 2

## Ingredients:

- 1 can coconut milk
- 1 teaspoon of cocoa powder
- ½ teaspoon vanilla extract

- 1 tablespoon Erythritol

## Directions:

1. Mix up together the coconut milk, cocoa powder, and Erythritol.
2. Add vanilla extract and stir until smooth.
3. Place the coconut mixture in the ice cube molds and place in the freezer for 30 minutes.
4. Then transfer the frozen coconut milk mixture in the blender and blend until smooth.
5. When you get smooth and solid ice cream mixture – it is cooked.

## Nutrition:

Calories 281, fat 28.7, fiber 2.9, carbs 7.3, protein 2.9

# NOTE

CPSIA information can be obtained
at www.ICGtesting.com
Printed in the USA
BVHW041056170521
607436BV00015B/721

9 781801 934527